BEGINNER'S GUIDE

TO

MICROSOFT FORMS

2022

BEGIN TO LEARN AND SUCCEED

BRIAN SMITH

COPYRIGHT

Printed in the United States of America

© **2022 by Brian Smith**

TABLE OF CONTENTS

INTRODUCTION

Microsoft Forms is one of the applications in 365 and new online software or surveying tool that allows you to easily create individual custom quizzes, surveys, polls, questionnaires, how to respond in any web browser or mobile device, and analyze those responses in minutes. The author of the form quickly sends to target audience who respond with ease in using either desktop, laptop, or mobile devices. The author can use the built-in analytic tools to analyze the results and further explore Microsoft Excel tables when the audience starts to respond.

Although several other surveying tools are available to create surveys, Microsoft Forms serves as an easy and quick way to do that. This beginner's book will serve as a guide in using Microsoft Forms which students, employees, business owners, etc., can use.

SECTION ONE – GETTING STARTED

1.1 CREATING A NEW FORM

The first step in using Microsoft Forms is to Login into the Microsoft account using your registered **Username** and **Password**.

To Access Microsoft Forms

- Go to the Application Launcher located on the top-left of **the Microsoft 365** page.
- Select **Forms** from the list of applications.
- **Microsoft Forms** web app will open.

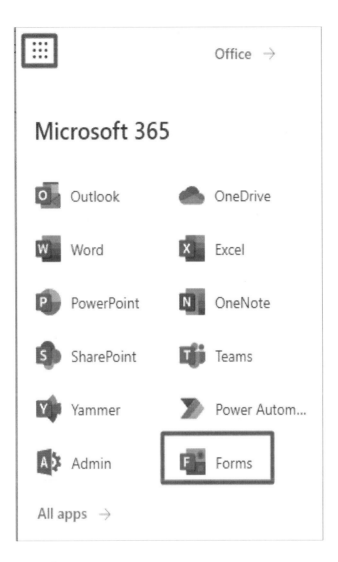

To create a Microsoft Form

- Click **New Form** directly to create a new form.

1.2 ADDING A FORM TITLE

It is always good to add a title to your form for easy reference. You can add **titles, subtitles,** and even **images** to your form.

To add a title

- Click the form title; this brings out a page for you to add your title, description, and even photo.

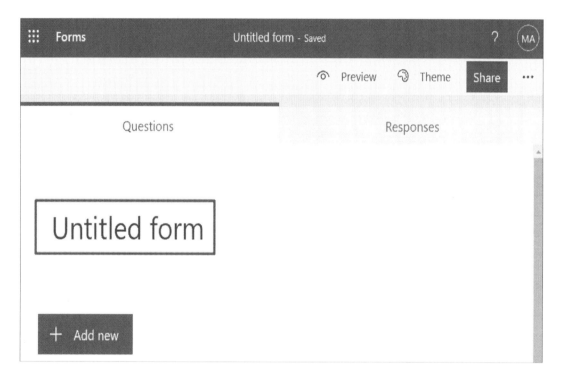

- Click the **Insert Image** button to add a photo to the title area of your form.
- The page looks like the one below.

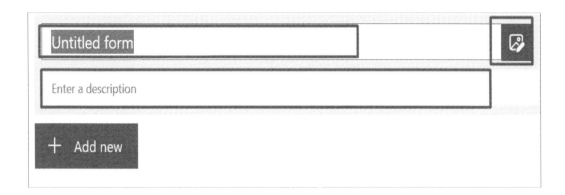

- After giving the name, description, and picture, the survey page looks like the one below.

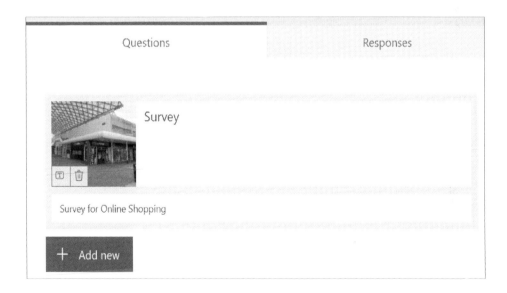

SECTION TWO - ADDING QUESTIONS TO A FORM

You can do this by using the **+ Add new** button on the question tab. There are different types of questions to add that will be discussed below.

To add a question to your form

- Click the **+ Add New** button .
- From the list of eight different question types, select the question type you want. You can see the other question types by clicking the down-arrow for more options.

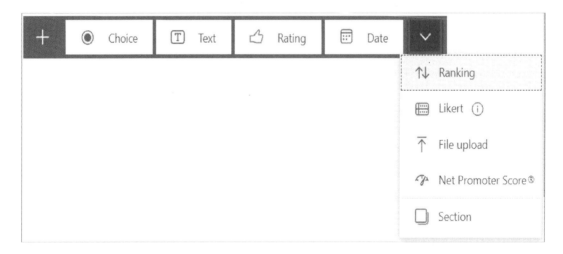

2.1 TYPE OF QUESTIONS

This section will look at the eight different question types and how to use them. Let us discuss in brief the eight types of questions.

- **The Choice** is used for questions with a preselected set of answers for the responder to choose from the options.
- **Text** – This type of question requires a text answer.
- **Rating** – This requires a rating in either stars or numbers.
- **Date** - The response to this question requires a date answer.
- **Ranking** – This requires the options of the questions to be in an arranged order.
- **Likert** – This type of question gives a range of answer options.
- **File Upload** – This type of question requires you to upload a file as an answer.
- **Net Promoter Score** – This type of question is required to measure customer experience and predict business growth.

2. 2 FIELDS AND SETTINGS COMMON TO ALL QUESTION TYPES

Some fields in the question area are general to all types of questions. These are;

2.2.1 Question

This is a text box area where you type your question, which will appear as a column header when you download your questions in an Excel spreadsheet.

2.2.2 Question Subtitle

This is a text area where you can enter any additional information related to the question. You can access it by clicking the more button to the right of the page. ⋯

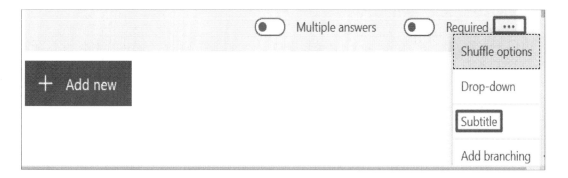

2.2.3 Insert Media

This is beside the Question text area, which appears when you click the question area. When you click, it gives you access to insert a media into your form.

2.2.4 Required

When enabled, this is a button that will require the person filling your form to answer the question, which, if not answered, the **Submit** button of the form will be disabled.

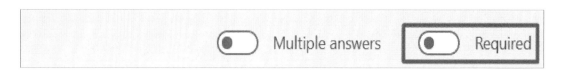

2.3 CATEGORIES OF QUESTIONS

Questions in Microsoft Forms are categorized based on the type of response required. We will discuss different categories of questions below.

2.3.1. Choice questions

This category of question allows responders to select an answer from a list of options. To create a choice question, select the choice question type from the list of question types. It is a must for the choice question type to have at least two options for the participant to choose.

To create a choice question

- After launching Microsoft Forms, click the **+ Add new** button, then click **Choice.**

- Click the question text box to add your questions.
- If your question requires a subtitle, click the more options button and select **subtitle**. Type your subtitle; this appears below the question text box.

- If you would insert a media, click the **Insert media** option button.
- If responders have to answer a question before they can submit the form, enable the **Required** button.

- Click the Options text box to add options to the question.
- Click the **+ Add option** button to add additional options to the question if you have more than two options.

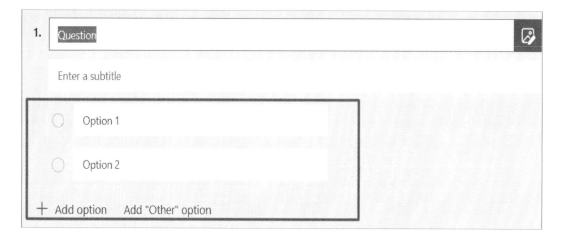

- Click **Add "Other" option** to add an option where the participant can type a response, bringing an option named **Other.**

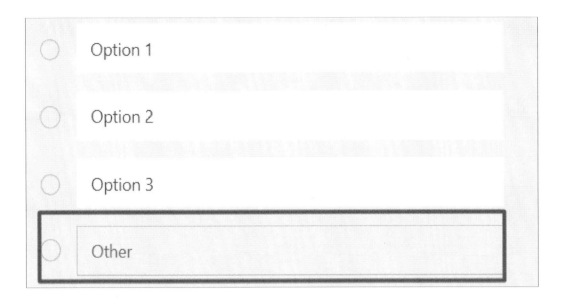

- Click **Multiple answers** to allow your participants to select multiple choices.

- If you want to rearrange the choices randomly, click the more options button 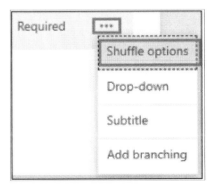 and click **Shuffle options**.

- To make the choices in a drop-down menu, click the More options button 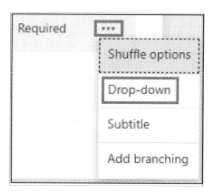 and select **Drop-down**.

2.3.2 Text questions

This type of question allows responders to type an answer while responding to the question. The answer to this question can be text or number.

To add text questions

- After launching Microsoft Forms, click the **+ Add new** button, then click **Text.**

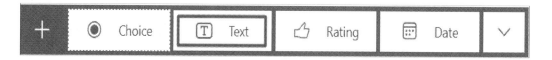

- Click the Question text box to type to question.
- You can click the Insert media option to add media to your form.
- Click the **Long answer** button to enable a larger text box for your question.

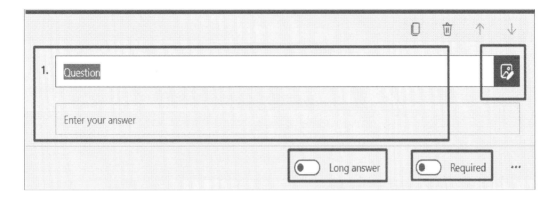

- To add restrictions to your form, click the more buttons and select **Restrictions.** This will force the participant to answer with a number.

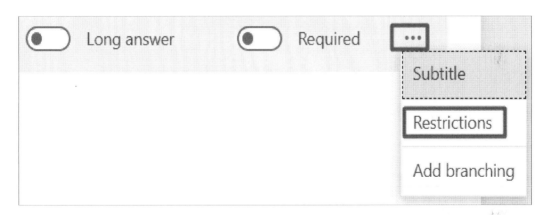

- When you click Restrictions, a drop-down menu appears to select the type of number or range you want to restrict the responder to enter.

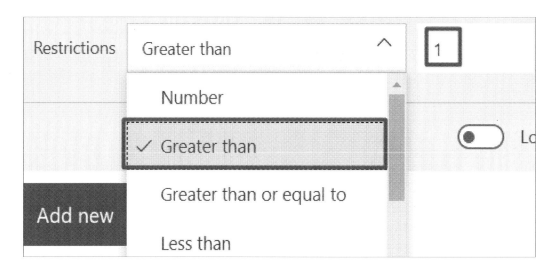

2.3.3 Rating questions

This question type gives the responder the ability to answer the question by providing a rating of several stars. You can change the rating from 5 to 10.

To create a rating question

- After launching Microsoft Forms, click the **+ Add new** button, then click **Rating.**

- Click the Question text box to add your question.
- You can add media to your rating question.
- Click the **Levels** drop-down menu to change the rating scale.
- Click the **Symbol** drop-down menu to select the rating type, either **Number or Star.**

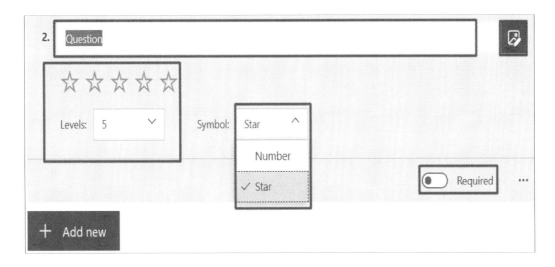

2.3.4 Date questions and answering a date question

This question type allows the responders to respond to date. When a responder is about to answer the question, a calendar pops up to select the appropriate date.

To create a date question

- After launching Microsoft Forms, click the **+ Add new** button, then click **Date.**

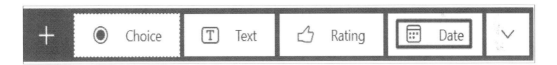

- Click the Question text box to add your question.

Answering a date question

The responder can answer this type of question only when the form is in a live state by selecting a date from a given calendar.

To answer a date question

- The responder can be able to choose the year by clicking the drop-down menu of the years.

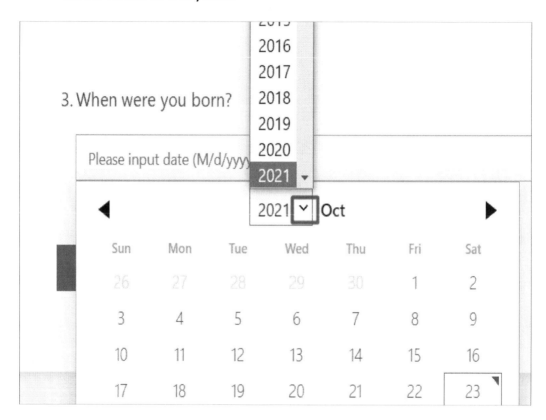

- They should use the left and right arrows to change the month in the calendar.

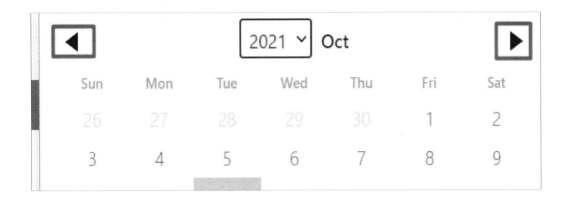

- They can select the day by clicking on it.

Sun	Mon	Tue	Wed	Thu	Fri	Sat
26	27	28	29	30	1	2
3	4	5	6	7	8	9
10	11	12	13	14	15	16
17	18	19	20	21	22	23
24	25	26	27	28	29	30
31	1	2	3	4	5	6

2.3.5 Ranking questions and answering a ranking question

This type of question allows the responders to rearrange the given options based on their ranking.

To create a Ranking question

- After launching Microsoft Forms, click the **+ Add new** button, then click the more options button.
- Click **Ranking** from the drop-down menu.

- Click the question text box to add your question.
- Click the Insert media menu to add media to your form.
- Type your options in the text boxes provided below the question.
- Click **+ Add option** to add additional options

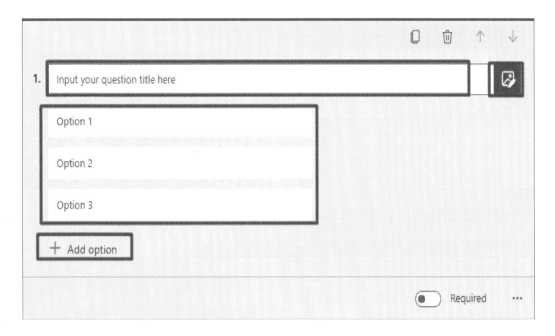

To answer a ranking question

- Move your mouse over the option you want to rank either up or down on the list.
- Click the associated up or down arrow attached to it to change its position in the list.
- Repeat for all other options.

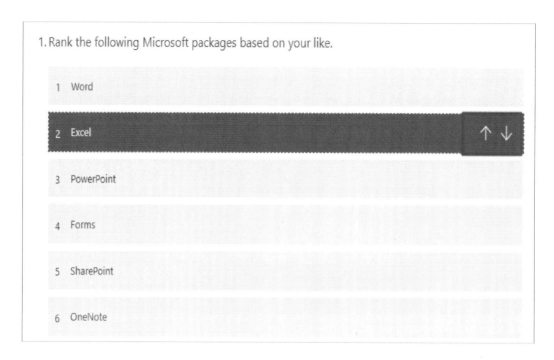

1. Rank the following Microsoft packages based on your like.

1	Word
2	Excel
3	PowerPoint
4	Forms
5	SharePoint
6	OneNote

2.3.6 Likert questions and answering a Likert question

This question type is often used in survey research and allows for a custom rating of your questions. The responders will be able to select a rating from the options provided for each statement.

To create a Likert question

- After launching Microsoft Forms, click the **+ Add new** button, then click the more options button.
- Click **Linkert** from the drop-down menu.

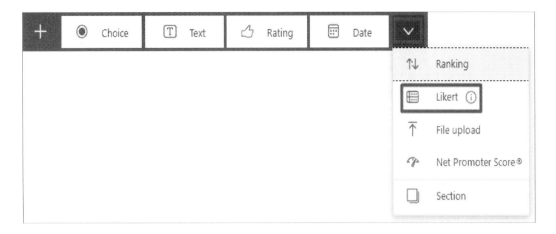

- Click the question text box to add your question.
- Click the Insert media menu to add media to your form.
- Click **statement 1** text box to add statement and repeat for **Statement 2.**
- Click **+ Add statement** to add additional statements.
- Click **+** sign at the end of the options to add additional options.

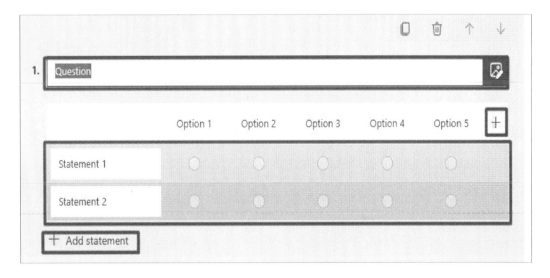

- Click the statements and type your statements in the corresponding text box.
- Click the options and type your options in the corresponding text box.
- If the options are too much for your question, click an option and

click the **Delete** icon to delete it.

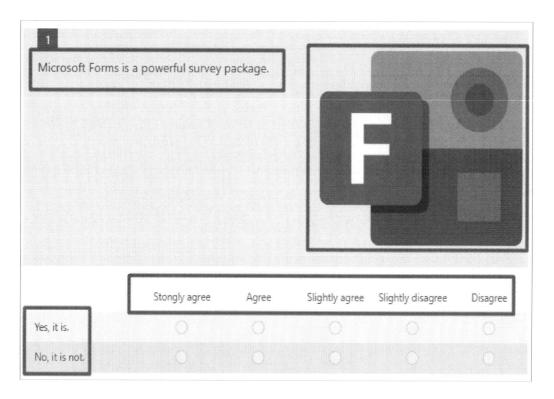

To answer a Linkert question

The responders only click on the radio buttons corresponding to the appropriate answer under the statements to answer the Likert questions.

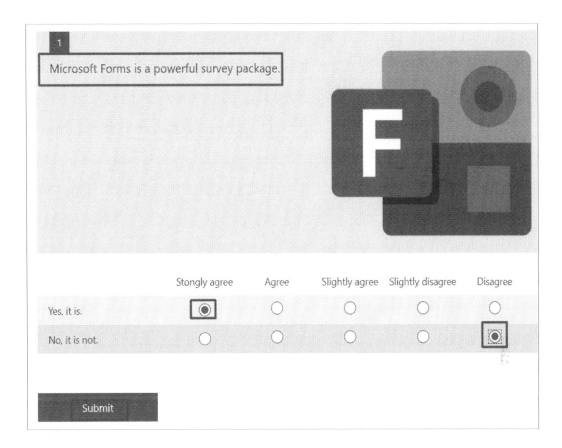

2.3.7 File upload questions and answering a File upload question

This type of question allows the responder to upload a file as an answer to the question. You can use this where a response is needed, and other types of questions cannot satisfy.

To create a File Upload question

- After launching Microsoft Forms, click the **+ Add new** button, then click the more options button.
- Click **File upload** from the drop-down menu.

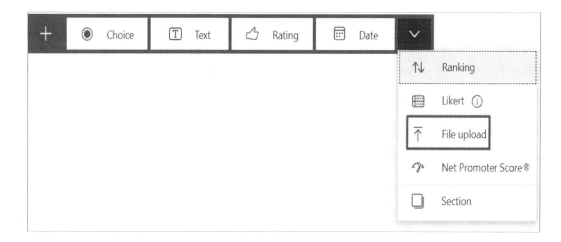

- Click the **File number limit** drop-down menu to specify the number of files a responder can upload.
- Click the **Single file size limit** drop-down menu to specify the limit for the size of files to be uploaded.

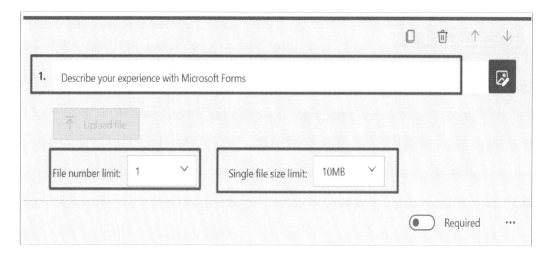

- Click the question text box to add your question.
- Click the Insert media menu to add media to your form.

To answer a File upload question

- Click the **Upload file** button.
- Select the file you want to upload. The chosen file will show below the question after uploading it.
- When you finish, click **Submit**.

1. Describe your experience with Microsoft Forms (Non-anonymous question ⓘ)

↑ Upload file

File number limit: 1   Single file size limit: 10MB   Allowed file types: Word, Excel, PPT, PDF, Image, Video, Audio

Submit

2.3.8 Net promoter questions and answering a Net promoter question
Organizations usually use this type of question to create a survey about their customers' satisfaction or how well they relate with their customers.

To create a File Upload question

- After launching Microsoft Forms, click the **+ Add new** button, then click the more options button.
- Click **File upload** from the drop-down menu.

- A default question appears once you create this type of question with you can change.
- You can also change the scaling by clicking the appropriate text boxes to enter your desired text.
- Click the Insert media menu to add media to your form.

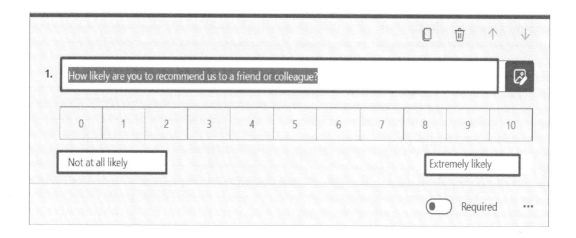

To answer a Net Promoter Score question

To answer a Net Promoter Score question, type the responders just have to click the number corresponding to their answer for a particular question.

2.4 SECTIONS

Sectioning is very important when creating a lengthy form that has to be well organized and reordered. The questions can be organized into multiple sections, which responders attend to a long-form arranged into smaller parts. Sections also help when you are using branching on your form.

To add a section

- After launching Microsoft Forms, click the **+ Add new** button, then click the more options button.
- Click **Section** from the drop-down menu.

- Click the text boxes to change the title and description of the Section.

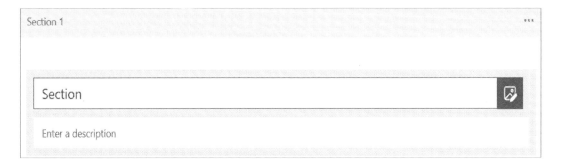

To duplicate, move or remove a section

- Go to the right of the Section and click the more options button (...)
- Click **Duplicate section** to duplicate the Section.
- Click the Move section to move your Section.
- Click **Remove section** and select **Just Section** to remove just the section header or **Section and questions** to remove the Section and all questions attached.

SECTION THREE - MANAGING QUESTIONS

The questions in your form can be copied, deleted, or reordered.

3.1 COPYING A QUESTION

To copy a question

- Go to the question you want to copy. A menu appears above the question.
- Click the **Copy question** icon to duplicate the question above the current question.

3.2 DELETING A QUESTION

To delete a question

- Go to the question you want to delete. A menu appears above the question.
- Click the **Delete question** icon to delete the question.

3.3 REORDERING OF QUESTIONS

To reorder your questions

- Go to the question you want to reorder. A menu appears above the question.
- Click the **up or down** arrow to move the question up or down to reorder it.

3.4 BRANCHING

Branching is a logic that allows questions to change according to responses to specific questions. In a survey with branches, questions appear only if they are relevant to the responder. If the questions do not apply to the responder, they are redirected to a different set of questions, or a set of questions will skip altogether. It works well with the Choice question type.

Note: Make sure all your questions are created before you start branching.

To add Branching

- Click the More options button (...) at the bottom right of each question.
- From the drop-down menu, click **Branching**.

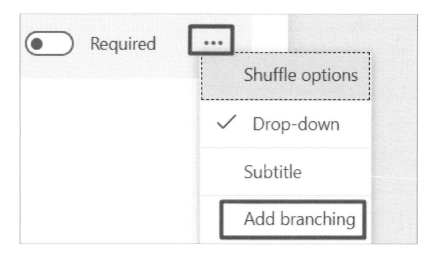

- Click **Go to** the drop-down menu corresponding to an answer to enable an answer to the branch.

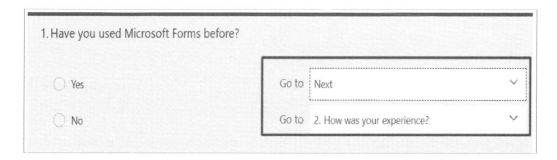

- Select your following action from the drop-down menu attached to the next question.

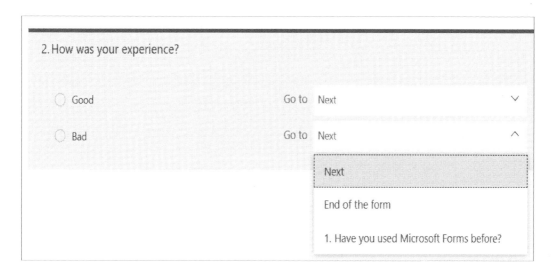

- To reset all your branching, click the More options button at the top Branching options and click **Reset**.

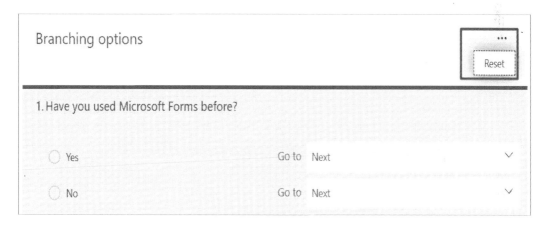

- Click the **Back** button above **Branching options** when you are done branching.

3.5 PREVIEWING YOUR FORM

This is looking at your form to see what it will look like to your responders.

To preview your form

- In the navigation bar and click the **preview** button.

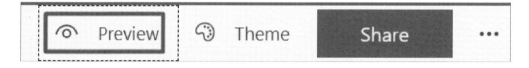

- Click either **Computer** or **Mobile** previews at the upper-right corner of the form to switch between computer and mobile view.

- Click the **Back** button for you to return to the form edit screen.

SECTION FOUR – FORM SETTINGS

Settings allow you to set additional functions for your form.

4.1 ACCESS SETTINGS

- Click the More options button (...) at the upper-right of your form.
- From the drop-down menu, click **Settings**.

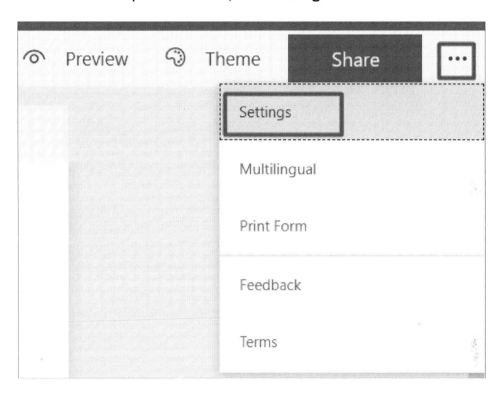

4.1.1 Who can fill out your form?

- This section allows you to choose who will respond to your form. **Anyone who has the link can respond,** or **Only people in my organization can respond**.
- Check the box beside Record Name to record the **responders' name**s and **email addresses** as an added column to the Microsoft

Excel spreadsheet containing the responses. When left unchecked, it will submit forms as anonymous.

- Checking the box beside **One response per person** will limit one responder to submit only one form.

4.1.2 Options for responses

This contains five response options that can be enabled or disabled by clicking the check box beside it.

- When **accepted responses** are enabled, responders can start to submit their surveys.
- When the **Start date** is enabled, you can give a specific set date and time to start allowing responders access to your form.

- When the **End date** is enabled, you can give end responders a specific set date and time to access your form.

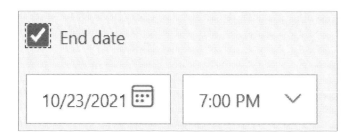

- Selecting **Shuffle questions** will rearrange your questions randomly for each responder.
- Enabling the **Customize thank you message** makes you customize the message a responder receives after submitting their response.

4.1.3 Response Receipts
- Enabling **Allow receipt** of response after submission will send an email to the responders after submitting the form.
- Enabling the **Get email notification of each response** will send an email to you as the form's owner each time a responder submits their form.

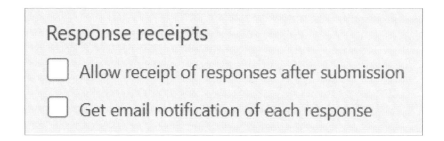

4.1.4 Form Themes
Microsoft Forms come with a default green color background which you can change to your favorite color.

To change your form background design, color and add images

- Go to your navigation bar and then click the **Theme** button.
- Choose from the available colors and backgrounds; this will be automatically added and saved.
- Click the last **+** button to add your image or customize the theme color.

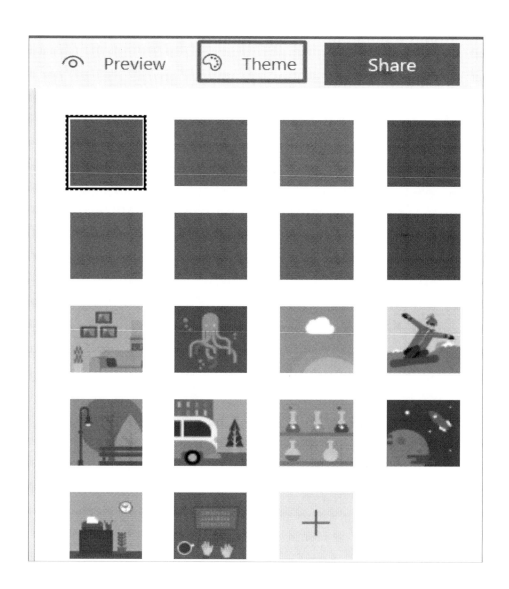

SECTION FIVE - SHARING OF FORMS AND COLLECTING

RESPONSES

You can use a lot of options available for you to share your form after creating it.

To start sharing your created form

- In your navigation bar, click the **Share** button.
- Select the type of people with whom you want to share your form.

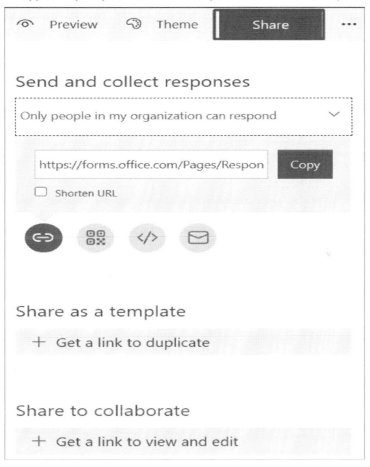

5.1 SHARING METHODS

There are four different ways that you can share your form

5.1.1 Link

This is the default and first option you can use. A link is generated for you in a text box.

To share a form using a generated Link

- Click the **Copy** button to the right side of the link text box.
- Paste the copied link in an email, document, or any other destination.

5.1.2 QR

This means a Quick Response. A QR code is generated for the responder to scan with their smartphone or tablet to access the form when using this option. Click the Download button to save the code to your computer. This option is most suitable for signage or other printed material.

5.1.3 Embed

This method generates an embed code that you can copy and paste into a website. Click the copy button beside the link text box to copy the generated embed code.

5.1.4 Email

This option automatically opens a new email in outlook containing the form's link to add your recipients' email addresses to send to them.

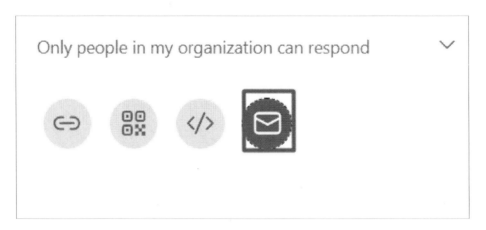

5.2 OTHER SHARING OPTIONS

There are two more additional sharing options available for building and collaboration.

5.2.1 Share as a template

This link, if generated, will share a duplicate of your form without the responses. The recipient of the form will click the link and add the form to their Microsoft Office 365 account.

To share your form as a template

- Click the **+ Get a link to duplicate** below the Share as a template heading.

- Copy the link by clicking the **copy** button to paste it into an email, 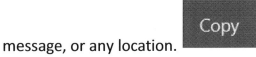 message, or any location.

- Click the **Delete** button to delete and disable the link. 🗑

- When trying to delete, a confirmation will appear. Click the **Remove link** button.

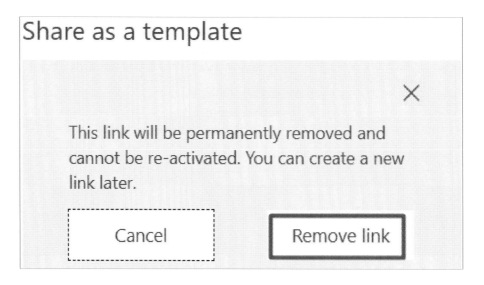

Share as a template

This link will be permanently removed and cannot be re-activated. You can create a new link later.

Cancel   Remove link

Note: For you to share as a template again, you must generate a new link.

5.2.2 Share to collaborate

Sharing with this method enables the recipient to have access to edit your form. It is good that the link is disabled after distributing the form to prevent and disable any accidental changes from the recipients.

To share to collaborate

- Click the **+ Get a link to view and edit** below the Share to collaborate heading.

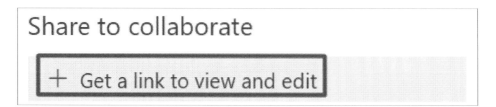

Share to collaborate

+ Get a link to view and edit

- Click the **Copy** button to copy your link and paste it into an email,

message, or any location.

- Click the **Delete** button to delete and disable the link.

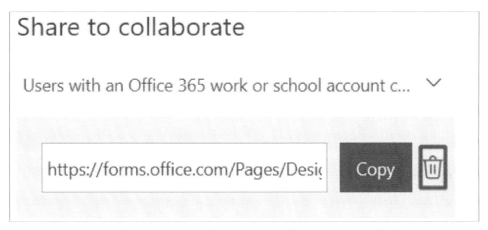

- When trying to delete, a confirmation will appear. Click the **Remove link** button.

Note: For you to share to collaborate again, you must generate a new link.

SECTION SIX - WORKING WITH RESPONSES

6.1 VIEWING RESPONSES IN FORMS

There are two ways to view your responses. The fundamental way is to view your responses through office 365 Microsoft Forms, and the other way is to view your responses through the Excel workbook that Microsoft Forms create by default when you create your forms.

To view your responses in the Microsoft Forms in Office 365

- Go to **Forms** in Microsoft Office 365.
- Click the form you want to view its responses.
- Click the **Responses** tab for the form.

- Scroll down the page to view the response details for other questions. Click the **More Details** below each question to see the list of responders for that question.

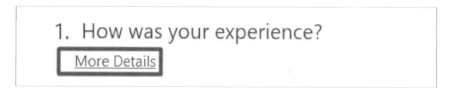

To view the result by the participants

- Click the **View Results** button on the responses page.

- On the screen, view participants' responses by using either the left or right arrows or the Respondent drop-down menu.

- To delete or print the participant's response, click the options menu (...).

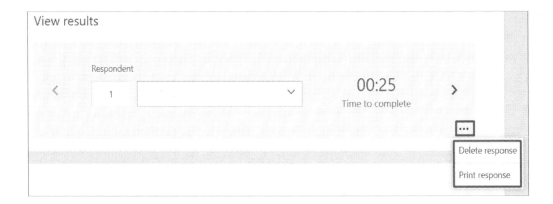

To delete all responses

- On the responses, page click the options menu (...).
- Click **Delete all responses**; this will delete all responses in the tab but not delete the Excel workbook's responses.

To Print summary

- On the Responses, click the options menu (...).
- Click **Print summary**; this will print the summary view of the responses in the responses tab.

To create a summary link

- On the Responses, click the options menu (**...**).
- Click **Create summary link,** and this will create a link to the summary.
- Click the **Copy** button of the link to paste it where you want it to be.

- When you finish with the link, click the **Remove Link** button to disable the link on your form.

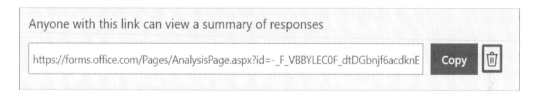

6.2 VIEWING RESPONSES IN EXCEL ONLINE

Whenever you create Microsoft Forms, it will create an Excel workbook automatically in your OneDrive.

To view your responses in Excel

- Click the **Open in Excel** button on the Responses page.
- The link will open in Excel Online.

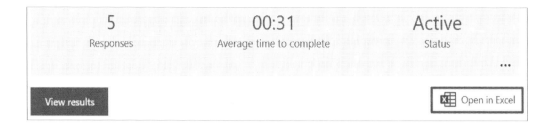

6.3 DELETING A FORM

Sometimes when you finish using your form, you may wish to delete it from your list of forms.

To delete a form

- Login to your Microsoft 365.
- Click on **Forms.**
- Click **All My Forms** below the page.

- Look for the form you want to delete.
- Click the More options button (...) of that form.
- Select **Delete**; this will move the forms to the Recycle bin.

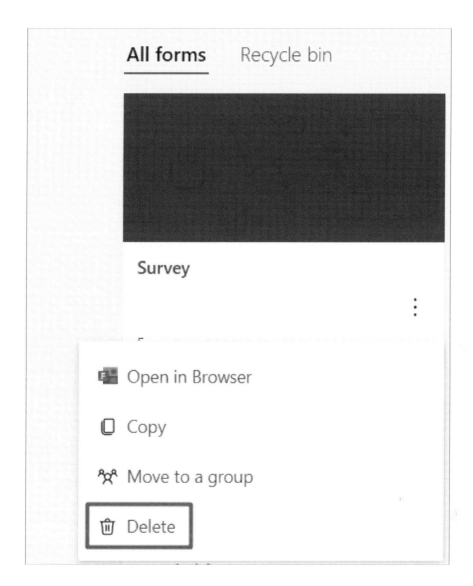

All forms   Recycle bin

Survey

⋮

🖳 Open in Browser

🗐 Copy

👫 Move to a group

🗑 Delete

To restore your deleted form

- Click the **Recycle bin** button.
- Click the More options button of the form you want to restore.
- Click **Restore** to restore your form to your All Forms tab or **Delete** to delete them permanently.

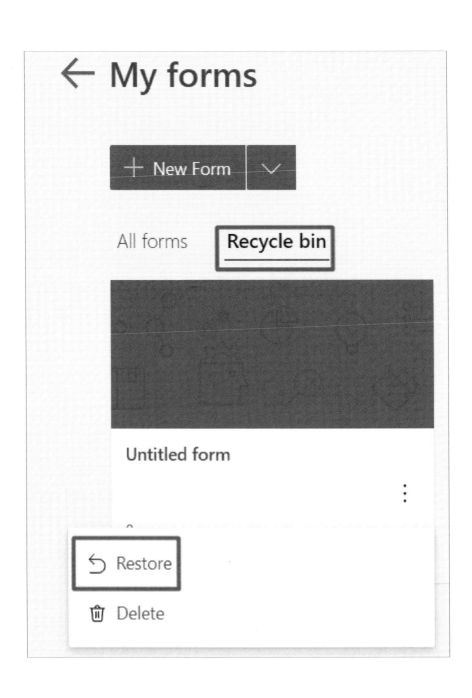

CONCLUSIONS

Microsoft Forms is a simple tool that students, teachers, industries, and other businesses can create custom quizzes, questionnaires, surveys, polls, and many other feedback requests. Creating a form and inviting people to respond to it using any web browser or even mobile phone is simple with Microsoft Forms. The received results can be used for evaluation and easily exported to Microsoft Excel for additional analysis.

Printed in Great Britain
by Amazon

84903829R10034